AF228598

POKÉMON

SATOSHI TAJIRI

Paige V. Polinsky

Big Buddy Books

An Imprint of Abdo Publishing
abdobooks.com

abdobooks.com

Published by Abdo Publishing, a division of ABDO, PO Box 398166, Minneapolis, Minnesota 55439.
Copyright © 2022 by Abdo Consulting Group, Inc. International copyrights reserved in all countries.
No part of this book may be reproduced in any form without written permission from the publisher.
Big Buddy Books™ is a trademark and logo of Abdo Publishing.

Printed in the United States of America, North Mankato, Minnesota
102021
012022

Design: Emily O'Malley, Mighty Media, Inc.
Production: Mighty Media, Inc.
Editor: Liz Salzmann
Cover Photographs: amirraizat/Shutterstock Images (phone), Hethers/Shutterstock Images (card),
    Mighty Media, Inc. (Tajiri), Nicescene/Shutterstock Images (Pikachu), Vladimir Borozenets/
    Shutterstock Images (ball)
Interior Photographs: BlurryMe/Shutterstock Images, pp. 25, 29 (top); CTRPhotos/iStockphoto,
    p. 9; I and J Photography/Shutterstock Images, pp. 15, 29 (bottom); inmedialv/Shutterstock
    Images, p. 13; Michael Overkamp/Shutterstock Images, p. 5; Rachel Lovinger/Flickr, p. 11; RG-vc/
    Shutterstock Images, pp. 23, 28; RICHARD DREW/AP Images, p. 19; Sarunyu L/Shutterstock
    Images, p. 21; Sergei Bachlakov/Shutterstock Images, p. 7; Steven Groves/Flickr, p. 27; United
    Archives GmbH/Alamy Photo, 17

Library of Congress Control Number: 2021942814

Publisher's Cataloging-in-Publication Data
Names: Polinsky, Paige V., author.
Title: Pokémon: Satoshi Tajiri / by Paige V. Polinsky
Description: Minneapolis, Minnesota : Abdo Publishing, 2022 | Series: Toy stories | Includes online
    resources and index.
Identifiers: ISBN 9781532197123 (lib. bdg.) | ISBN 9781098219253 (ebook)
Subjects: LCSH: Tajiri, Satoshi, 1965---Juvenile literature. | Pokémon (Game)--Juvenile literature. |
    Inventors--Juvenile literature. | Toys--Juvenile literature. | Pokémon Company International--
    Juvenile literature.
Classification: DDC 338.47688--dc23

CONTENTS

CHAPTER 1

DR. BUG

Satoshi Tajiri was born on August 28, 1965, in Tokyo, Japan. As a child, Satoshi liked to look for bugs in the forest. He carefully studied each one he found. Satoshi's friends called him Dr. Bug.

As Satoshi grew older, he began playing **arcade** games. No one knew he would later **develop** one of the most popular video games in history!

Satoshi particularly
enjoyed catching
stag beetles.

GAME FREAK

Tajiri's love of gaming continued. In 1983, he decided to write a magazine for gamers. He called it *Game Freak*.

The magazine was a huge success! Tajiri found several other people to help him produce *Game Freak*. They and Tajiri felt most video games were not very good. This led Tajiri to another idea. What if he made his own game?

With *Game Freak*, Tajiri created a community for gamers. Today, Pokémon fans have a similar community and meet to play and share their knowledge!

'ZINE TO SCREEN

Tajiri created a game called *Quinty*. Tajiri showed *Quinty* to video game company Namco. To his surprise, Namco approved it.

Namco **released** *Quinty* in 1989. Tajiri and the *Game Freak* magazine team were now a game **developing** company. Tajiri continued using the name Game Freak for the company.

Namco also created the *PAC-MAN* game.

CHAPTER 4

YOSHI

Tajiri's next idea was *Pokémon*, a game with monsters. He showed it to game company Nintendo. However, Nintendo asked Tajiri to make a different game instead. So, Tajiri created *Yoshi*. Nintendo **released** *Yoshi* in 1991. Its success proved that Tajiri was a talented game **designer**. So, Nintendo agreed to release *Pokémon*.

Nintendo's headquarters is in Kyoto, Japan.

CHAPTER 5

TWO GAMES

Tajiri and Game Freak created 150 monsters for *Pokémon*. The monsters were also called Pokémon. The team made two games so players could trade to collect all the Pokémon!

The games were called *Pokémon Red* and *Pokémon Green*. On February 27, 1996, Nintendo **released** both *Pokémon* games in Japan.

Pikachu is the most well-known Pokémon. The Macy's Thanksgiving Day Parade often includes a Pikachu balloon.

CHAPTER 6

TRADING CARDS

The *Pokémon* games sold well. But Nintendo needed to offer something new to keep players interested.

Nintendo worked with **manga publisher** Media Factory to create the Pokémon Trading Card Game. It came out in October 1996. It featured the same Pokémon that were in the video games.

Today, there are more than 11,000 different Pokémon cards.

CHAPTER 7

MORE MEDIA

Nintendo continued creating new products featuring Pokémon. The Pokémon TV show **aired** in April 1997. The next year brought the first Pokémon movie. Both were big hits in Japan. Also in 1998, the Pokémon TV show and video games were **released** in the United States. American **audiences** and gamers loved them!

In the United States, the main character in the TV show and movies is Ash Ketchum. Pikachu is his sidekick.

CHAPTER 8

NOT JUST A GAME

Soon, there were Pokémon products everywhere. There were Pokémon backpacks, toothbrushes, and more.

In April 1998, Nintendo and Game Freak formed the Pokémon Company. It would **manage** the Pokémon **brand**. In December, the Pokémon Trading Card Game was **released** in the United States.

Pokémon were featured at the 2000 American International Toy Fair.

MORE GAMES

Handling the many Pokémon products kept the Pokémon Company busy. Meanwhile, Nintendo **released** several new *Pokémon* games in 1999. These included *Pokémon **Pinball**, Pokémon Snap*, and *Pokémon Yellow*. These games gave fans fun new ways to enjoy Pokémon.

There is an entire store just for Pokémon products at the Kansai International Airport in Japan.

CHAPTER 10

MONSTER MAKERS

Game Freak and Nintendo continued to **develop** new *Pokémon* games. On October 14, 2000, Nintendo **released** *Pokémon Gold* and *Pokémon Silver* for the Game Boy Color.

These new games had the same **themes**, goals, and Pokémon of the first games. But *Gold* and *Silver* also **introduced** 100 new Pokémon!

Game Boys are handheld gaming devices manufactured by Nintendo.

POWER
GAME BOY COLOR
B
A
Pokémon
Red Version
©'95'96'98 GAME FREAK inc.
DMG-P-PKGS-NHAU
POKéMON
TRAINER
Nintendo GAME BOY
Pokémon
Nintendo
Pokémon
Gold Version
Nintendo

CHAPTER 11

READY, SET, GO!

Pokémon remained popular through the early 2000s. During this time, more people were getting **smartphones**. Nintendo worked with Niantic Labs to create a *Pokémon* app.

Pokémon GO came out in 2016. As users walk around, different Pokémon appear on their screens based on where they are in the real world.

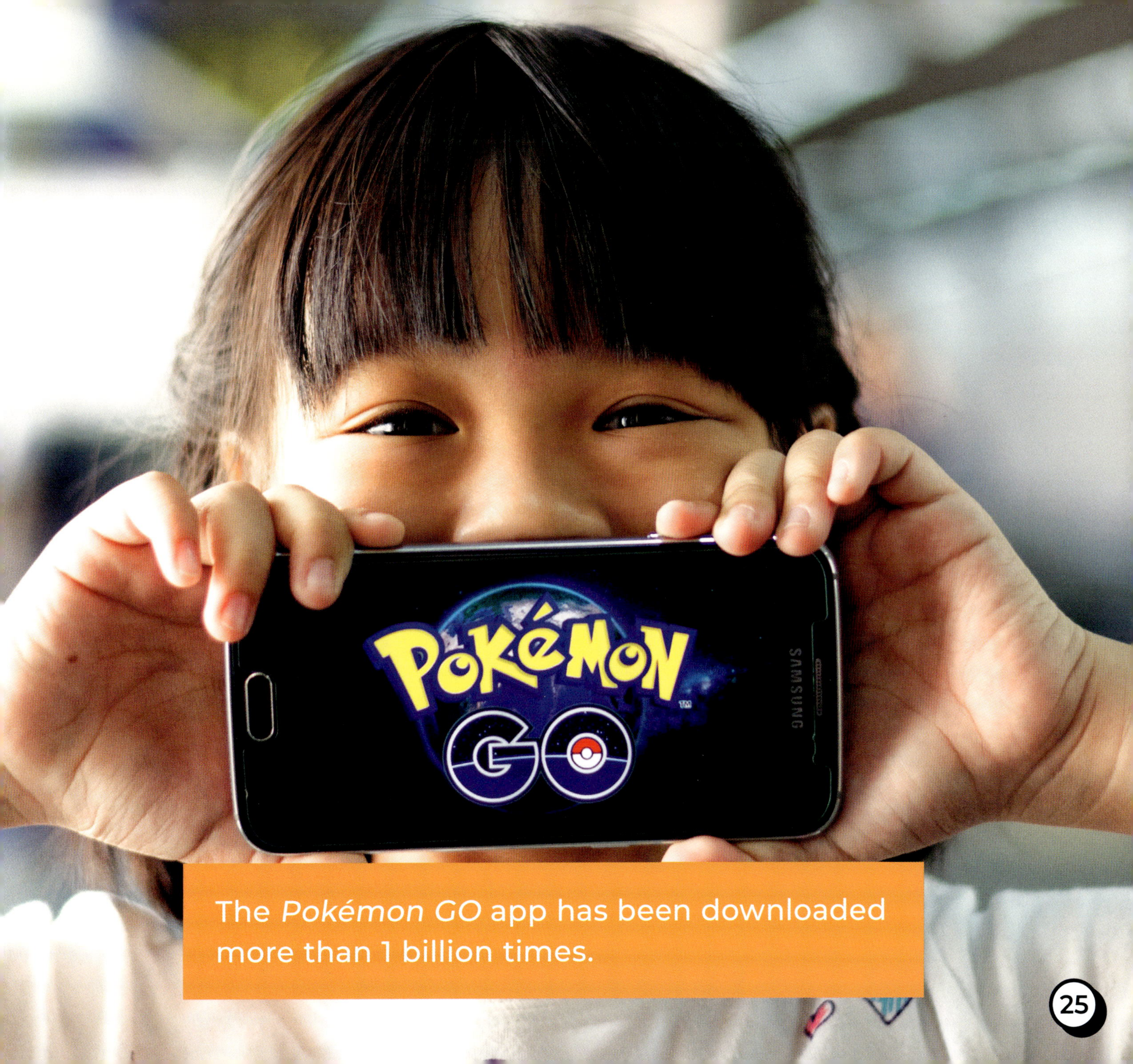

The *Pokémon GO* app has been downloaded more than 1 billion times.

POKÉ-NOW

New *Pokémon* games continue to be **developed**. Many of them **introduce** even more Pokémon. By 2021, there were 898 different monsters.

Over the past 20 years, the joy of catching and trading Pokémon has not faded. It seems certain that gamers will keep working to collect them all!

Collectors can buy special boxes and carrying cases for their Pokémon cards.

1996

Pokémon Red and *Pokémon Green* are released in February. The Pokémon Trading Card Game is released in October.

1965

Satoshi Tajiri is born on August 28 in Tokyo, Japan.

1989

Tajiri's first video game, *Quinty*, is released by Namco.

1983

Tajiri publishes his first issue of *Game Freak*.

1991

Nintendo releases Tajiri's game *Yoshi*.

1997

The Pokémon
TV show first
airs in April.

1999

Several new *Pokémon*
games including *Pokémon
Pinball*, *Pokémon Snap*, and
Pokémon Yellow are released.

2016

Pokémon GO is
released.

1998

The Pokémon TV show, video
games, and trading cards are
released in the United States.
Nintendo and Game Freak
form the Pokémon Company.

2000

Pokémon Gold and
Pokémon Silver are
released in October.

GLOSSARY

air—to show on television or play on the radio.

arcade—an amusement center that has coin-operated games.

audience (AW-dee-uhns)—a group of people that listens to or watches a show.

brand—a category of products made by a particular company and all having the same company name.

designer (dih-ZINE-ur)—a person who plans how something will appear or work.

develop—to create something over time.

introduce—to present or announce something new.

manage—to have control of and make decisions about something.

manga—a Japanese comic book or graphic novel.

pinball—a game in which a metal ball rolls around a slanted surface and bounces off obstacles.

publisher—someone who makes and sells games, books, magazines, or newspapers.

release—to make available to the public.

smartphone—a cell phone that can connect to the internet.

theme—the main subject of something such as a book, movie, or game.

INDEX